MW01240933

DO IT NOW!
TOMORROW MIGHT BE
TOO LATE.

GINETTE K. FOTSO

Ginette K. FOTSO

TABLE OF CONTENTS

INTRODUCTION

Many of us have been there. You've been granted 30 days to plan for a term paper- but you're not really working on the paper before its due date. This can be regarded as Procrastination.

There are many definitions of procrastination, which will be displayed more detailed in the next section.

How many of us are putting off what we should be doing today until tomorrow?

Whenever we practice procrastination, it destroys our productivity —Thus killing our dreams. Just think for a minute: what can you possibly achieve (which is worth accomplishing) if you fail to act? You will eventually live in a pig pin if you put off cleaning your home, not to mention the health problems that may arise from poor maintenance.

My Personal Experience On Procrastination

I was a procrastinator during a long time, full of good projects and ideas but full of postponing them to wait for the good and perfect time and perfect conditions to get them perfectly done. This willing of perfectionism exposed me to always shift my tasks and ideas for the future. In the meanwhile, I could see people around me also having ideas and projects and making them come into reality, in such a way that they could earn a living with, while I had great ideas popping up into my mind almost every week or month, but doing absolutely nothing out of them, if it was not to postpone them and wishfully think about their future realization.

I identified procrastination during many months in my daily routine, though I was comfortably letting it be, without daring to take concrete actions to crush it.

The real change does not come when you identify procrastination or recognize you are procrastinating; knowing the steps of getting out of procrastination will not help you either. It is taking actions to performe those steps that will give you the victory over it.

When I identified I was procrastinating, instead of doing everything to get out of it, I even procrastinate on the day that I'd come out of that mood, spending all the time thinking of that glorious day when I'll finally get out of it and will perfectly achieve all my projects; The biggest problem was that I did not see that glorious day in a near future. I was shifting it until the day I began to despise that condition I was in: Full of babies (projects), but keeping my legs closed to avoid the pain (process, challenges, critics) of giving them birth. Then it was clear to me: doing so, I would either kill them all (the projects) or will die at the end with them in my belly (my mind) if I do not release them.

Then I decided to start doing them now. This decision raised a war of questions in my head, a war between what I just decided and what mister procrastinator wanted to decide for myself:

-"Start doing them now? Really?"

-"In fact from your many, many and various projects what will you be able to start with?"

-"By the way- what makes you believe you can start them now, that you more time-sucking responsibilities in your job?".

-"Don't exhaust yourself. You don't have much time now, take time for your job and to rest at the end of the day; in some years when you'd have stored enough money, you can quit your job and you'll have a lot of time for your personal projects or anything else."

But like a bell it kept ringing in my head: "stop thinking- start acting! You have to choose something to get started with."

Then I started thinking about many other people who might be in the same situation, thinking about how many babies (projects, ideas) could have been imprisoned in many "bellies" because of procrastination, which I decided to help crushing that out of their lives, mainly by sharing my own experience on this matter. I first had to work myself on geeting out there before I try to motivate others to believe that it is possible. Today I'm thankful that I'm out of it and to be a witness that is possible with your decision, discipline and determination.

WHAT IS PROCRASTINATION ?

Procrastination is the act of delaying or postponing tasks to the last minute or exceeding their time limit. Some researchers define procrastination as a form of failure to self-regulation characterized by an irrational delay in tasks despite potentially negative consequences. Procrastination is otherwise described as intentionally and habitually putting off what should be done now. Too many people are fooling themselves into thinking that procrastination is only happening without any actual intervention or feedback. That is not valid, however. You ought to take an involved part to procrastinate. You are knowingly engaging in and triggering your downfall because you realise something has to be achieved- so you agree not to do so.

Procrastination is not, in most cases, a sign of a major problem. It is a common tendency that most people may have at some points or areas of their lives. Delaying tasks can be understandable to some extent, but irrational delaying is what makes procrastination a problem to deal with.

Regardless of how well-organized and committed you are, chances are where you have found yourself frittering away hours on trivial pursuits (seeing TV, updating your Facebook or WhatsApp statuses, shopping online) when you should have spent that time on your work, on your personal or school-related projects.

Whether you are postponing the completion of a work project, avoiding homework assignments, or ignoring household chores, procrastination can have a major impact on your job, grades, and your whole life.

Don't Let Procrastination Kill Your Dreams Of Being A Success

The simplest and most effective solution for procrastination is to take the necessary action where necessary. When it's time to go to the gym or work out, most people procrastinate but report feeling better after going to the gym or exercising. Every time you postpone, you are at times left to feel guilty of having not done the right thing; But on the contrary, every time you do the right thing in due time, you will always have a great feeling of satisfaction, which can also be a great source of motivation to keep acting.

Procrastination is a road to unsuccessful grades and poor job performance that can lead to job losses. Nobody wants these things happening to him- right?

Before you would like to go further and deal with procrastination, you should maybe first know whether it applies to you or not.

Recognizing Procrastination

The first phase in resolving procrastination is the knowledge and the nature of procrastination. You can't get an answer to a question you have never noticed or even asked yourself. Same for a medical issue. You don't receive the care you need unless you understand and identify the concern first, so you can pass on to the problem medically.

Establish "Why" You Procrastinate

Understanding the "why" behind your procrastination brings you closer to getting over it. Let's say you're putting off your house cleaning. That it's because you enabled things to get so out of control that it's getting difficult for you, and you just want it to go down. Typically procrastination takes place whenever there is no pleasurable task that needs to be done. Most of us have no problem doing things that please us: we almost tend to distance ourselves from pain and draw close to pleasure.

Causes

Remember that time you thought you would have a week left to complete a project that was actually due the next day? How about when you chose not to clean your apartment because you "hadn't felt like doing it right now?"

We also think that tasks are not going to take as long to finish as they are going to, which may contribute to a false sense of self-confidence because we feel we still have plenty of time to complete them.

One of the biggest contributing factors to procrastination is the notion that we must feel inspired or motivated at a given moment to work on a task.

The reality is that if you wait until you're in the right frame of mind to perform certain tasks (particularly undesirable ones), you'll probably find that the right time simply never comes along, and the task never ends.

Many experiences show that the best way of adding pressure to your life is to wait until the deadline is pre-eminent. If you are a student, or a worker, or whatever you do and have a deadline on it, you surely have already noticed at least once that doing it on time will free you from stress whereas postponing it will give you a double charge to carry: The first charge being the continuous "thought" that you have something to do, the second one beeing that you haven't done it yet.

Other factors which cause procrastination are the following:

Academics

procrastination between students is particularly pronounced. A meta-analysis published in the Psychological Bulletin in 2007 found that a whopping 80 percent to 95 percent of college students regularly postpone tasks, particularly when it comes to completing assignments and coursework.

Some significant cognitive disruptions that lead to shifting tasks, according to researchers. What students tend to include:

- They overestimate the amount of time they have left to perform jobs.

- In the future, overestimate how inspired they would be.

- Underestimate how long it will take to complete some activities.

- Incorrectly assume they need to be in the right spirit to work on a project or task.

Fear of success as a possible cause of procrastination?

What if the thing we fear the most is not to fail, but to succeed- or even to succeed exceedingly and beyond our expectations?

The thing we possibly fear the most is that we could be competent and proficient beyond measures. Some people postpone their task just because they are afraid of the success that could be the result of their actions if they move ahead now.

We must also admit that success in some cases can be so big an hefty that it carries more responsibilities in our lives, so it's almost easier not to start doing anything to succeed now and keep on living with the motto "one day - one day, someday i will".

Another Cause: Are You A Perfectionist?

As you surely have heard it in many motivational speeches, you should 'dream big', 'dream of perfection', and there in nothing wrong in that..

.. but please: start with little things, with little steps which you take and complete everyday. When you are hungry and want to eat, and finally you get a delicious meal before you; sitting down, admiring the food and thinking about all vitamins that it may bring to your body, postponing the action 'start to eat' will not make the meal more delicious nor will it quench your hunger and give you the strengths and vitamins you need. Start with one spoon; if it's too hot then wait; blow on it; then take another spoon; eat it; stop sometimes and enjoy the flavor, you can even lick you spoon if you want ☺ ; take another spoon until you finished it up.

It's nearly the same scenario when you have a project or an idea : Don't sit down and admire it, dreaming about how big this could be if 'one-day' it comes to be realized. Instead, start working on it, day by day, when it's too hot (things are becoming difficult), then take a breath, relax, stop and appreciate every effort and step you have already achieved, come back the next day and continue your journey through your task or project.

If we just sit and wait until all our uncertainties and fears of failure are gone, if we wait for the perfect time to be perfect and to do you that perfect thing, we could end up doing it very late...or we will end up never doing them at all; A person who waits to know everything, who waits for circunstances to be favorable and perfect, might probably end up doing nothing other than waiting; in the best case, he will end up doing things with a huge delay and much more pressure.

More Reasons Why We Procrastinate

We often come up with several excuses or rationalizations in addition to the reasons why we procrastinate to justify our behavior. Several reasons why people procrastinate includes:

- Not knowing what needs to be done

- Not knowing how to do something

- Not wanting to do something

- Not caring if it gets done or not

- Not caring when something gets done

- Not feeling in the mood to do it

- Being in the habit of waiting until the last minute

- Believing that you work better under pressure

- Thinking that you can finish it at the last minute

- Lacking the initiative to get started

- Forgetting

- Blaming sickness or poor health

- Waiting for the right moment

- Needing time to think about the task

- Delaying one task in favor of working on another

If you can recognize yourself in more than 6 of the points stated above, don't ignore them- you have to deal with it on time.

FIVE TYPES OF PROCRASTINATORS: WHICH ONE ARE YOU?

We are all procrastinating on certain tasks and aims. Some people procrastinate on learning for examinations or writing a thesis. Others postpone writing a book or start their own business. Or regular exercise and fixation of their diet. And if you've ever beat yourself for not completing the job, remember you 're not alone.

This chapter will display which type of procrastinator you might be and what you can do to get out of it. If can see yourself in one of these types, you can start fixing it much easier by dealing with the specific root that potentially causes it.

Honestly I could recognize myself in almost all types of procrastinators- which was another sign that I must quickly crush that thing out of my living zone.

This having been said, If we look at the key factors why people always push off things, we can roughly describe five specific forms of procrastinators.

The Five Procrastinator types:

1. The Wishful Thinker

Poor planning skills are among the most common reasons for procrastination. This type of procrastinator sets big and daring goals regardless if they are realistic or measurable, without any thought. They just scribble down on a piece of paper their new year's resolutions and hope the universe will make them real. Unfortunately, in most cases, that is not how it works out. Let's look at the common mistakes made by this type of procrastinator.

Are You Setting Crappy Goals?

For this sort of procrastinator to set a target that is not simple and observable is a clever trick. It's a way of not holding yourself accountable and having your work postponed without negative consequences. If you can't quantify nor qualify the target, after all, there's no way to know whether you missed it.

Here are some vague goals:

- *Lose weight*

    That was typically me. When I was still in the shifting mood, I rarely settled exactly how much weight I wanted to lose, or which weight

I exactly want to reach. I would always formulate approximative wishes like " I want to reach **around** 75 Kg", in other not to be accountable if I just manage to reach 77 kg- which is still around 75, right?

- *Start a business*

  You have one or several business ideas, but you would plan to start or launch them- someday when you will have more time, more money, more confidence, etc.

- *Learn to play the guitar*

  I remember that I bought a guitar when I was a procrastinator, but after two weeks I send back because it was too big and the resonance was not pleasant to my ears- another whole story. I did not hurry to buy another because I had no qualitative or quantitative goal on what I wanted to reach while learning, which made me also not feel guilty or accountable for anything

As you may see, all the examples stated above have no clear goal or target; there's no way to know whether you've achieved those goals. For instance- based on those same examples- you have no idea of:

- how much weight to lose exactly at which time?
- Which weight do you exactly want to reach at the end?
- How far you want to go while learning guitar; Which songs to be able to play in a given period?
- What type of business to start? What is the idea behind? What is the plus-value or which problem will it be solving?

To be as unspecific as that is a wide door opened to procrastinating and ending up doing nothing concrete and measurable.

Are you hoping the goal will achieve itself?

Another error is not to establish a simple course of action to accomplish that goal. Whatever the target is, you must still do the job step by step.

This is another scam used by this form of a procrastinator. If we don't set a goal, a target, a measure, there's no way in which to see how you do the job and how far you progress every day. When you don't have a measurable step or progression, there's no way to say whether or not you're procrastinating.

Thinking of Your Future Accomplishments Everyday?

This is also a typical habit of wishful thinkers. They could spend days and months thinking about their project. Thinking of "that day" where they wish so much their projects will be accomplished . But they would never take time to work for one hour on it.

If you keep doing nothing, "that day" might never come. You better start to act now, because some weeks or months from now on you may wish you had started today. Every single action counts, every single day counts. Stop dreaming, stop counting the days and make each of your days worth to be counted as a fully and purposely achieved day.

Never got enough time to work on the goals?

And if you determine the next step, if you don't set aside the time for it, you would not make much progress. You can not foresee a miraculous freeing up of your calendar and making more flexibility for your latest goal. So excuses like: I was too busy today, or my cat got sick, are easy to use.

A Solution for The Wishful Thinkers

If you frequently make any of the above mistakes, it's a sign that your planning needs to get better.

Here's a simple way you can use to set a goal you want to achieve:

- *Focus on the specific result that you want—* Imagine having already accomplished the target, and imagine what it feels like. Make it visual, as if you were watching it on a film screen. What would you look like after achieving that goal? How does that make you feel? How would you perceive the others around you?

- *Create your strategy—*If the goal is to know your vision, the strategy is about the steps of action which will take you there. What would you need to do every day to make the goal come true? Build a list of all the actions and measures you would need to follow next. Many books propose various of strategies which can be helpful, but to be honest I couldn't find help for myself there. Rather I lost more time trying to apply each and one of those strategies, which were simply not suitable for me. You are the one knowing your project, your goal, so you are the best person to create a steps and actions to reach that goal. But of course if you do not have a goal or do not have an idea of what you want to achieve, there is no "fixed-written-miraculous" strategy who will help. First get a clear idea or project. Then work on a strategy.

- *Schedule time to work on it* — To ensure you are executing your plan,intentionally set aside a specific time for it. Book your calendar online. Commit to turning up and do the job daily. Think about what excuses might arise if you don't do the job every day and get rid of them before you even start.

In my case I had to deal with how I used my time. When I started the process of "doing things now", setting up strategies, booking my calender online and assigning time to tasks did not work at first glance.

During the time I booked my calender for a task, I sat, started it, but in parallel, I was thinking of too many other tasks or always trying to look at my phone every twenty minutes. The result is that I always ended up not doing what I planned to do. I had to be violent on this , and I started with a deal which I called "CCs" (concentration- challenges): The challenge consisted of working concentrated during 30 minutes consecutively, then 1, 2, 3 hours- without touching my phone or trying to think about something other than the actual task.

I always had a great feeling of satisfaction anytime I would take a step forward on this challenge. I trained myself on this habit and by today, when I settle to work on something, I work on it on time and in deeds.

- *Set a clear deadline*—By which time do you expect to reach the goal, based on your strategy? Is it a month, a year, five years? Make sure you keep track of your progress, setting milestones along the way. Check if you're on track every week to reach your goal. If not, which adjustments would you make to the plan to keep you on track?

If you are a wishful thinker, it's time to stop dreaming about your goals and work to accomplish them. Between the dreamers and the accomplisher, there is a little bridge called action- and I'm sure you know this; so please, do act!

As I started to set quantitative goals in my life that I could achieve within a clearly defined time, it was really huge a victory for me. But this was just the first step, because most of the time you don't do things just for yourself, but also for others' satisfaction. Therefore acting or being busy is good, but there is much more above that. Don't just act to act. Got it?

In fact: you may work for yourself, but most of the time you would be working for someone else (your boss) or would be selling your services to others, etc. Therefore one thing that I want to emphasize on is to add **quality** to what you do or to the work you want to deliver. What does it bring to people (your boss, your customers, etc.) if you always deliver things **at the right time** but with poor quality or content?

This will, of course, bring nothing if it's not tarnishing your self image and reputation- which would surely make your business live for just the while as you deliver that poor service. To be (extremely) productive at bad or unimportant thing can be as worse as not to be productive at all.

2. The Last-Minute Junkie

"I'm going to finish it tomorrow"- that's most probably your best though if you are a last-minute junkie.

Of course! You are so special, you feel so wise and talented to be able to still accomplish the work at latest as possible, isn't it?

This type of procrastinator leaves it all for the last possible second. The problem of being a last-minute-junkie is that you end up having too little time to finish the job or you have to pull an all night. Your valuable research is thus not quite as successful as it should be.

Please seize for yourself the depth of the following statement: procrastination is a great betrayer and time-stealer: it won't only teach you how to perform one week tasks in one night, but also how to perform one night of task in one week.

Here are some of the last-minute junkie features:

I Like Working Under Pressure!

One excuse they use to delay the work is that at the last minute, they will be more efficient. They enjoy the pressure to know that the deadline is coming and that they have to finish it fast. But doing it all quickly also implies bad performance.

Surely, It Will Be Easier Tomorrow

"Today, I simply have no motivation. That's either too hot or too cold. I 'm going to be in a better mood tomorrow. "

Whatever the particular excuse is, they rationalize delaying the work for a hope of a better future. Yet the future is full of the same issues. Tomorrow, you'll have just as many reasons to procrastinate as today, since the "day after" will still be "tomorrow".

Fun First, Work Later

Junkies of the last-minute love quick and simple tasks. They start with something fun, and later in the day, they put off the harder work. Consequently, at the end of the day, there never seems to be enough time left for the hard work.

In my secondary school time, I was a real last minute junkie, and I always succeeded in it, which gave me more self-confidence that I was a "super-student" because I needed less time than my fellow classmates to submit the same work, and was among the best -if not the best- at the end.

I kept this habit over the years in many areas of my daily routine, shifting things and succeeding at the end in doing them in shorter time and under pressure.

But that was without taking some factors into account: Pressure would grow as I am growing in age and responsibilities. When I was in secondary school, I was under my parent's cover, so I did not have to stress over anything than the school. While growing I accumulated more responsibilities, and shifting them all (or almost) to the day before the deadline would just bring much more pressure on me, which is absolutely not healthy in the long-term.

Think of your health- do what you can to today and free the space in your calendar for another things.

A Solution for The Last Minute Junkies

If you're a last minute junkie and want to beat procrastination, you've got to stop thinking about your future self as another person. Stop deluding yourself that you'll be more motivated, have more time, or will be focused tomorrow.

If you rely on your achieved previous results in "last-minute-doing", it's clear you won't take this as a serious matter, cause you've always succeeded. But if you want to get out of this last-minute-mood, you need to begin with the most important task first — no matter how hard it is. Free your morning calendar, don't open your email or social media, don't look at your simple tasks. Only continue with the most important or difficult one.

What helps in performing difficult and hairy tasks is breaking them down into smaller piecesand fix the goal that you can achieve. Figure the very first step and write it down. Do it on the previous night, too. This means you already know what the first move is when you wake up so you can get cracked without distractions.

If you continue with the difficult task, even if it's a little piece — and complete it — then you've got the momentum moving. You'll feel more productive, and all the other tasks will feel like a reward for the day (because they're easier).

3. The Resourceless

You 're the resourceless procrastinator when you use a lack of anything and not doing the work.

- *Time*—Right now, you are simply too busy. You have to wait until you have more time on your hands to begin to work on the goal.

- *Money*—It's just too expensive, you can't afford to start now. Let's just wait for the financial situation to get better.

- ***Knowledge/competence*** —How should I achieve that objective when I don't know anything about it? Where should I start anyway?

- ***Contacts/experts*** — I just don't have the right contacts to make this happen. I need to wait a little longer before the right people show up.

A Solution for The Resourceless

There is an abundance of opportunities in this day and age. Using any of the above reason isn't a justification not to start.

You can find a cheap way of eating better, exercising, starting a business, or doing a hobby. All you need is to do more research and stop using money as an excuse. On the internet, you can learn pretty many things for free.

Time is never the issue, either. We all have the same timescale. The question is, are you prepared to prioritize your goal and not procrastinate in the time you already have?

As for contacts, we 're more connected nowadays than we have ever been. You can find experts to help you on any subject, as long as you are willing to look at it.

4. The Perfectionist

Perfectionism give birth to procrastination as soon as the desire for excellence is not more the purpose, but the fear of failure clothed with fineness. Most perfectionists wear it as an honourable badge. It is perceived as being of so "good quality".

There is a difference between doing quality work and wasting time on insignificant details, though. In the details, most perfectionists get lost and procrastinate on the truly important work.

Here's how perfectionism can bring you into trouble:

All or Nothing

Perfectionists believe there is no point in getting off to a start unless your work is perfect. But if you wait for the alignment of all the stars before you start — you'll simply never.

It's yet another lie to assume the best conditions. Any of the hard work is sloppy. To get done, they require lots of trial and error.

Losing Track of the Big Picture

Usually, perfectionists begin with a grand plan and a great aim.

But pretty quickly, they lose control over where they're headed because the irrelevant specifics get them bogged down. Ultimately, all these tiny information just bog you down and don't help you make any changes.

A Solution for the Perfectionist

The antidote for the perfectionist procrastinator is to repeat the mantra "Progression matters, not perfection."

If you focus solely on the perfect result, you lose track of the progress that you make every day. And if you don't make many changes every day, you'll run out of energy and start procrastinating pretty fast.

Even if you're finishing just 50% of what you intend to do today, it's far better than doing nothing. Begin by figuring out what is important. What is the main purpose of the work you are doing, and how do all the steps of action contribute to that?

Use the rule 80/20. Ignore all the details that only 20 percent of the results bring. Focus on the tasks you want to achieve the 80 percent result.

5. The Intimidated or Self-doubter

Another cause of procrastination is fear of your goals and tasks. This type of procrastinator prefers postponing the work than directly confronting the fear.

Let see the types of fears which cause procrastination:

Afraid to Make a Mistake or Fail?

Are you having thoughts like –"what if I continue and mess it on?" –"I probably would have felt worse than not starting at all"?

So instead of taking a risk, you are postponing the work, hoping it will get easier somewhere down the road, and you'll feel more confident.

I'm Not Good Enough

Many people are scared of putting themselves out there. They 're worried about what other people's thinking. For even thinking to start an ambitious goal — impostor syndrome, they feel like a fraud.

They procrastinate with learning to be as good as being pleasant to everybody, instead of starting now. The following are some of their favorite questions:- Perhaps reading more about the subject will make this easier? -Perhaps training two or three more months will make the result acceptable and pleasant for everybody?

My Task Is difficult, Big and Hefty.

You may be afraid because what you want to do is too hard. Too far away from your comfort zone?

Maybe you tried it in the past and epically failed?

From my personal experience that I'll be narrating in the next lines, I could learn that it's not because things are big or difficult that we do not dare to face them, it is because we do not dare that they become difficult for us.

In fact, I am among those who think that nothing is difficult. Instead: it is either our knowledge on one topic which is our limitation, or we are so afraid to deal with the topic. Medecine is not difficult; Robotics is not difficult; Mechanics is not difficult; but if i do not have (or want to acquire) any knowledge in those particular fields, or i dare not because i think there are big and difficult topics, then they will become difficult- even if in reality they are not.

In my profession, there are very complex and complicated functions of vehicles control units to develop in other to ensure vehicle and drive safety in critical situations. During the first months of my work, as I was seeing the zeal and commitment on how my colleagues where talking about those functions, the first and only information that I (consciously or not) choose to store in my mind is "this might be very difficult, this might be though, I may never be able to understand those functions."

I pertinently knew that I had to take time, sit and have a deep look in some of those functionalities that I will be using in one way or another. But fearfully, I kept postponing this event. I did not dare to start learning and working on those functions, I was even afraid of having deep headaches when I would start working on them.

From time to time, I would ask for very little and superficial informations to my colleagues regarding some functions, not even wanting them to go deeper into their answers because I was not ready to receive, ready to understand (an irrational fear of not understanding what I haven't even try to understand).

I kept postponing until one of those days where I was already in the process of crushing procrastination out of my life. I decided to sit and have from myself a deep look into those mysterious functionalities. After about two hours of concentration, I was reallymvery disappointed.

Disappointed and a bit ashamed of myself. My eyes suddenly started burning and watering, and I told myself: "What a mess"! Actually I would have been the one explaining those functionalities in deep details to my whole team. Those functionalities are purely derived and made out of mathematical physics and boolean algebra for electronics circuits used in digital technologies! And digital technology is one field that I loved and comprehended the most during my studies, from the first semester on.

In fact, my digital technology professor noticed my interest and passion from the very first lecture, as I was trying to question and understand every single 'how' and 'why'. He also noticed at the end of the semester, how deep i understood the topic, so as to be able to solve what he always mentioned to be "hard-hitting exercices", such as to hinder students from having full marks. I would rather say this was his strategy to differentiate the ordinary learning student to the student that really researches and understands the topic.

From the second semester to the end of my Bachelor program, the professor trusted me to support him in teaching digital technologies to first and second semester students, helping them to resolve and submit their exercises and laboratory, to correct their exam copies, etc.

If I was able to understand those basics of digital technology, there were no reasons that I could not understand the functionalities related to my work, even if there seemed hairy and 'advanced', i.e. more complicated. But procrastination made me not to settle and deal with those topics on right time; irrational fear made me think at the beginning that I could not understand so far (provided that many colleagues testified to have needed many weeks and sometime months to understand them). However, I was able to understand quite well.

If you are going or have gone through something similar, find in the following lines some pieces of advice that may help.

A Solution for The Intimidated/Self-doubter

Here's the thing — fear, if you just wait, never goes away. With time or with reading more about it, you won't become more confident.

The only way to get rid of fear is by directly confronting it — putting it into the work, failing, and not giving up. In reality, perseverance is what creates your self-esteem. But not to dare or to give up will rather lower your self-esteem and make you feel you are not able.

When they first started, nobody was a genius. At first, they all suck. Just look at your favorite authors, athletes, or celebrities in their early careers. Everybody had to begin with the basics and learn with trial and error.

And to be truthful: **Who says you cannot do it?** The following story illustrates quite well how we are sometimes the only ones doubting about ourselves, thus lowering our limits and thinking **we cannot.**

In the job I do, I sometimes have to run safety-critical tests in customer cars with multiple control units. A single person can perform those tests but, provided the complexity, it is highly recommended that they are performed with two people in the car. The deadline for showing the customer the test result was in three days -a Thursday- and on Monday my colleague got sick for the whole week, that same week in which the safety critical tests should be done. "I'll never be able to do this alone"- That was my first tought. Other colleagues won't be able to help me; Only my sick colleague and I were trained to have solid knowledge of safety and security in the whole team. "Even if I know how critical it could be if the tests are not performed until Thursday, I'll never be able to do this"- That is what I kept thinking. "You're in bad traps" – "how are you going to install all the electrical equipment alone"- "you might make a mistake and connect a cable wrongly"- "even if you install the equipment properly, you can get a safety-critical failure while testing and not just that, you can have a failure that leads to a deadlock or a complete vehicle shutdown". This seemed to me just to be too much, so much that I wanted to write that day to my boss and say I'm also sick, which would have been a big threat for the company fame.

As a Christian, I also knew that lying not a good option. Then I said "Lord, you should give me the strength to handle this". I know You're not going to install all the equipment in the vehicle, or do the test for me, but give me the strength and diligence to manage that. Then I opened the training documents on safety tests again at my workplace.

I read those documents again as if I were a new employee, so that i could refresh any single details that I could have forgotten. Then I went to the car, carried out the first test, the second, the third, the tenth, and they all failed. I couldn't comprehend why they actually failed — I figured out that of course.. I wasn't smart enough to handle it alone. It's was just a joke that I even tried it — but on the other hand I was so proud that I could at least set up the circuitry in the car and drive it the the test-track; I was so proud that I was able to undo the mistakes occurred while driving some tests, I was so proud of many single steps that I could manage alone.

But my joy was just for a short moment-I 'm happy for myself-what about the customer? Tomorrow they are expecting a successfully driven test!!! Then I was getting tired and decided to take a short brake. Meanwhile I was thinking: if I've gone so far with the test , that means I can do it successfully till the end — why have I failed — although I feel like I've done it all right? Where have I gone wrong? I just randomly opened my mails. I saw a message from the Test-tool support team, saying that there are some updates to be made in the new tool version before testing. It was just about a checkbox that needed to be unchecked. I opened the tool and updated accordingly. Then I went to my digital test-result-recorder: all tests previously marked as "failed" were marked as "successful"- I couldn't believe my eyes and I decided to renew the same tests immediately; all tests were successful. So really- who says you cannot, if not you?

What Type of Procrastinator Are You?

The hard thing about procrastination is that it's caused by a lot of different aspects. Everyone doesn't have a single solution.

Looking at yourself and figuring out what is the root of your procrastination is tough. Most of us are very good at noticing other people's undoing of tasks shifting, but we've got a blind spot to our own challenges. Even so, there are chances you've recognized yourself as one or more of these procrastinator types.

Now you have a clear understanding of why it's so challenging for you to step on. To get rid of procrastination, you don't have to spend time reading unendless strategies or downloading a lot of devices or tools. Knowing your type of procrastination, you can concentrate on overcoming what id holding you back. You should halt putting stuff off and start working on it.

Putting stuff off is a common occurrence among all forms of procrastinators. We 're waiting to see something improve. To make the aim or mission harder, anything to alter.

But waiting never works, in fact, it does make things harder. Out of my own experience, I can say this with assurance: the longer you sit on your projects and do nothing, the more the procrastination gets serious.

The only cure is to begin to act. The first step is to identify exactly which of these challenges and excuses will hold you back and tackle it before it has a chance to manifest.

Think about what would happen if you don't ?

Where would you be if you kept putting off your targets in 10 years? What changes will you miss? How should you feel about gazing back at your life from now on for ten years, realizing you've gone on procrastinating every day?

Also, think about what would happen in the opposite case.

If you got rid of the excuses, how much more could you accomplish? How would you change your life if you were working for your goals? How should you feel about your life realizing that instead of procrastination, you have had ten years of productivity?

DEALING WITH THE ROOTS OF PROCRASTINATION: REASON PEOPLE PROCRASTINATE

This section includes a list of the specific reasons people procrastinate, mainly based on the psychological mechanism outlined in the previous section.

If you're wondering why you're procrastinating yourself, look through this list and try to figure out which of these procrastinating roots apply to you. Try to be reflective and honest with yourself while you do this since it is crucial to figure out the underlying causes of your procrastination if you want to be able to overcome it.

Remember that not everyone here would refer to you, so feel free to skip through and read specifically regarding the explanations you think may be important in your specific case.

1. Abstract Goals

When their goals are vague or abstract, people are more likely to procrastinate than when their goals are concrete and clearly defined. Targets like "get fit" or "start exercising," for example, are relatively vague and are therefore likely to lead to procrastination. By contrast, a goal such as "going to the gym on Monday, Wednesday, and Friday right after work and spending at least 30 minutes on the treadmill running at high speed" is concrete, and is therefore much more likely to lead you to act.

Besides, remember that apart from the absence of a simple meaning, many variables may render a target sound vague. For example, goals that are perceived as highly improbable are also perceived as relatively abstract, according to the construal-level theory. This implies that if an individual feels it impossible that they can accomplish a particular objective, it will allow them to see the target as theoretical, which in effect can raise their chances of procrastinating on it.

2. Rewards That Are Far In The Future

People also procrastinate on activities correlated with incentives that they will earn just a while after finishing the assignment because people prefer to underestimate the importance of bonuses that are far out in the future, a concept known as temporal discounting or delay discounting.

For starters, it's easier to discount the value of getting a good grade on an assessment while that test is still weeks away compared to when it's just days away, which is one of the reasons people fail to complete the necessary tasks right before the deadline.

Accordingly, when people choose to engage in activities that reward them in the short term, they often display a present bias, at the expense of working on tasks that would lead to better long-term results for them.

Notice that the association between the time it takes to obtain a reward and the relative worth of that incentive is typically incoherent because of the discount rate increases with time. Essentially, this means that the further a reward is in the future, the less time it matters to increase when it comes to lowering the perceived value of that reward.

For example, while there is a big difference in how we value a reward that we can now receive compared to a reward that we can receive in a week, there is a much smaller difference in how we value a reward that we can receive in one year compared to a reward that we can receive in one year plus one week. Similarly, while there is a big difference between receiving a reward in one day compared within one year, there is a difference between receiving a reward in one year compared to receiving it in two years.

This phenomenon is called hyperbolic discounting, and it is contrasted with exponential discounting, which is a time-consistent model of temporal discounting, where an increased delay before receiving a reward always has the same effect on its perceived value, no matter how far it will be in the future.

Finally, note that, besides rewards, the same concept may apply to punishments as well. Essentially, this means the farther a possible punishment is in the future, the less it motivates people to act.

3. A Disconnect From Our Future

Often people procrastinate as they perceive their potential selves as separate from their present-selves, a condition is known as transient selves-discontinuity.

For instance, somebody might delay when it comes to eating healthy, even if their doctor tells them it's important because the harmful impact of their current diet will only begin to be a serious issue in a couple of years, which they see as the problem of someone else (i.e. their future).

This disconnection between the present and their future can cause people to procrastinate in many different ways. For the starters, that may lead them to believe that their present-self shouldn't have to care about the future because their future would be the ones that will have to manage any activities that they delay or contend with the repercussions of failure to finish certain tasks on time. Similarly, it can cause them to think that their present-self should not be bothered with doing things now if their future-self is the one who reaps the rewards of their actions.

4. A Focus On Future Options

Often people postpone doing steps right now since, in the future, they plan or expect to follow a more desirable course of action. This attitude can lead to long-term procrastination and persists even in cases where the person who procrastinates never ends up following their intended plan through.

For example, a person might avoid starting to practice alone at home, because they plan to join a gym and later start a detailed workout plan, although getting started now would still be beneficial and wouldn't prevent them from switching to a more serious workout plan in the future.

5. Optimism About The Future

Sometimes people procrastinate on tasks because they are optimistic about their future ability to complete those tasks. Such confidence can have to do with two key factors, namely the amount of time necessary to complete the task, or the innate ability of the individual to complete the task.

For example, students might decide to postpone starting with an assignment to a couple of weeks from now, because they feel there will be plenty of time to do it later.

In certain instances this type of anticipation will arise as a consequence of underestimating the time it would take to complete the tasks with questions; this tendency is known as preparation fallacy, and it may cause both procrastinators and non-procrastinators to believe that they can finish upcoming tasks faster than they actually would.

Similarly, after failing to get started on a job, an individual may agree to postpone it to the next day because they think they will be able to motivate themselves to work on it tomorrow, even though they have postponed the same job many times in the past in precisely the same way. In many cases, this form of optimism involves overestimating future abilities, and it is important to note that people who are prone to procrastination often promise themselves that when it comes to procrastinating on tasks, "things will be different next time."

6. Indecisiveness

People sometimes procrastinate because they are not in a position to make timely decisions. It can be a concern in a variety of cases, such as when an individual can not determine which course of action to partake in or when an individual has to make a particular determination before they can go on with their overall action plan.

An individual may postpone beginning a diet, for instance, because they can't decide which diet program to adopt. Similarly, an individual may postpone beginning their research paper because they can not decide what subject to write about.

Various causes usually make it more possible that one would overthink the scenario when attempting to make a judgment. This condition that is often referred to as "paralysis of thought" or "paralysis of preference".

From a practical perspective, the main factors to consider are the following:

- The more choices you have, the tougher you'll have to pick. The more choices you have to chose from, the more challenging it would be for you to compare them and determine which one is preferred.

- The more close the options are to each other, the more challenging it would be for you to pick. Essentially, the more comparable the choices available, and the closer they are in value, the more challenging it would be for you to determine which one is better, particularly in situations when there is not a single choice that is superior to the others.

- The more significant your decision is, the more complicated it would be for you to decide. Essentially, the larger the repercussions of making a choice, the easier it would be for you to finalize the choice, meaning that, you are more inclined to pause before making a major decision unlike making a minor decision.

Therefore, it is crucial to bear in mind that you end up depleting your energy to some degree each time you have to make a decision, particularly if you are prone to indecision. Accordingly, the more choices you have to make in a given amount of time, the more you are depleting your self-control ability, and the more inclined you are to postpone taking certain choices, at least before you get a chance to refresh yourself physically.

Lastly, note that this form of procrastination is generally referred to as decisional procrastination since it entails a delay in decision making.

7. Feeling Overwhelmed

Sometimes people procrastinate because they feel overwhelmed about the tasks they need to handle. For a variety of reasons, a sense of exhaustion may arise, such as having a single job that seems vast in scale or getting a large number of small tasks that add up. When this happens, a person may simply choose to avoid the tasks in question or may try to handle them, but then end up feeling paralyzed before those tasks are completed.

E.g., if you need to clean your entire house, you may feel overwhelmed by the idea that the chore would take so long and require so many pieces, in which case you might avoid getting started on it first.

Also good to know: often people procrastinate when they feel nervous about a job they have to perform. For instance, anyone who feels reluctant to review their bills may postpone doing so constantly, even though this avoiding does not trigger the issue to go away.

This issue may be especially troublesome in situations where the anxiety of an individual rises as a consequence of his procrastination, which can contribute to a reinforcement cycle in which someone feels nervous about a certain job, which leads them to procrastinate rather than do it, causing them much more nervous, which in effect leads them to procrastinate much more.

8. Task Aversion

People often procrastinate because they are unwilling to perform the tasks they need. For instance, if you decide to make an essential phone call to somebody (regardless if you like the person or not) and do not do it on time although nothing hinders you from doing so, you may end up procrastinating rather than getting it done.

Remember that many factors can render an individual unwilling to do a job in a manner that allows them to procrastinate on the job. For instance, a person may procrastinate because they perceive a task as frustrating, tedious, or boring, or they may procrastinate because they believe that there is a gap between the difficulty of the task and their competence, which means they feel the task is too difficult for them to handle.

9. Perfectionism

Perfectionism may contribute to procrastination in a variety of ways, such as making someone so frightened of making an error that they end up doing no action at all, or making someone so concerned about publishing something with certain defects that they end up reworking their project forever and ever rather than launching it when it's finished.

For instance, somebody might delay working on their book, because they want every line they write down to be perfect from the beginning, which makes them write nothing at all. Similarly, someone who's done writing a novel could postpone constantly sending it out for reviews, because they want to make sure it's perfectly perfect first, so they keep working through it, again and again.

While it is reasonable to want high-quality work to be created and published, the problem starts when the perfectionist aims for unattainable flawlessness, which causes them to procrastinate by giving them a valid excuse for unnecessary delays.

Notice in this respect that perfectionism does not necessarily contribute to procrastination, and there are also cases in which the perfectionism of an individual will cause them less inclined to procrastinate by forcing them to do a successful job and finish their tasks on time. As such, perfectionism is not inherently a bad phenomenon; it just contributes to trouble as it allows people to postpone something excessively since they are too concerned that their job is not flawless.

10. Fear Of Evaluation Or Negative Feedback

People sometimes procrastinate because they fear being evaluated or fear to receive negative feedback from others.

For example, somebody might postpone promoting a project they've been working on because they're worried about what other people would say about it.

In many situations, the concerns of individuals are irrationally inflated or unjustified in this respect, either because the chances of receiving negative feedback are small, or because the effects of that criticism are not as important as they sound.

Furthermore, remember that in some situations it is possible to make people less likely to procrastinate, by encouraging them to get their work done in a timely fashion, for fear of negative criticism. Whether this fear 's influence is positive or negative depends on a variety of variables, such as how nervous a person feels about the upcoming evaluation, and how comfortable they are in their ability to handle the task at hand.

Note that when you avoid the conflicts, the critics and ideas of others, because you think you want to keep the peace or you want to be in peace, know that you have started a war inside yourself. The best way to resolve is to be opened to the remarks, discuss them, to express yourself even if you fail to do so; It' s much more better than fighting with yourself.

11. Fear Of Failure

People sometimes procrastinate as they believe the projects they have to do would collapse. This fear of failure can promote procrastination in a variety of ways, such as causing people to avoid completing a task or causing them to avoid starting on a task first.

For starters, someone may be so afraid that their business idea would collapse, that they will end up working on it forever, without ever having it available to the public.

How fearful someone is of failure is generally related to how important the task in question is, so more important tasks are often associated with higher levels of procrastination, in cases where fear of failure is the driving cause behind the procrastinating person.

Furthermore, note that fear of failure does not always cause people to shy away from it. Rather, fear of failure promotes procrastination primarily when it reduces people's sense of autonomy, or when people feel unable to handle a task, they are afraid of failing to perform. On the other hand, when people feel well-equipped to handle a certain mission, fear of failure will function as a motivating factor that helps people to avoid procrastination.

Finally, keep in mind that fear of failure, perfectionism, and fear of negative feedback are all closely related to each other. Still, one does not necessitate the other, and any combination of these factors could influence a person. For instance, someone may be comfortable about their abilities to execute a job well but also worry about getting unjustified criticism from others, or they may be worried about failing at something even though nobody else cares about it.

12. Self-Handicapping and Self-Sabotage

People often procrastinate as a means of putting obstacles in their own direction, such that if they struggle, their shortcomings will be related to those obstacles rather than to their capacity. This behavior is considered as to be self-handicapping.

E.g., instead of preparing for a test, a student may procrastinate. After all, they think that they failed because of their procrastination, instead of understanding that they failed because they were unable to grasp the material well.

Let's figure this other real example: this kind of people who could postpone applying for a new position, even if they realized it was a fantastic opportunity for career development because they thought they didn't deserve to be in a better place in life. This is a self-sabotage, self-defeating behavior which is the enemy of your progress.

As a consequence of those defensive mechanisms, some procrastinators spend more time procrastinating when they think they are going to struggle when it comes to the task at hand, particularly if they fear as failure would adversely reflect upon them.

I can remember as I was still in secondary school. I hated doing sport, despite all benefits that it has for our health. I kept saying to my sports teacher that I was 'inept'. The sport teacher kept replying that unless I provide a medical certificate proving that - which my father never accepted to provide because from his point of view I should do sport as other students do. But only the fact that I had mentioned to my professor that I am inapt was a good reason for me to accuse my "inability" or "inaptitude" when I was not doing the movements and gymnastics the way they were prescribed, rather than accusing my incapacity or even my lack of will to do this. I was unconsciously sabotaged my capacities to be able to perform in sports. But I'm happy that nowadays, there is no week passing by without me doing some good physical exercice.

13. Low Self-Efficacy

Self-efficacy reflects the belief that a person has in their ability to achieve their goals successfully, and in some cases having a low degree of self-efficacy can cause a person to procrastinate. For starters, if somebody has a job they don't think they can manage, they may postpone getting started on it because they believe they 're most likely not going to finish it anyway.

Notice that persons may have various levels of self-efficacy about the different domains of their lives. For example, a person may have high levels of academic self-efficacy, but low levels of social self-efficacy, which implies that when it comes to academic tasks, they trust in their skills, but not when it comes social tasks.

Self-efficacy may also be related to specific roles or skills. In this context, the most notable among these is self-efficacy in terms of your ability to self-regulate your behavior to get you to complete tasks in a timely way. This is because the idea that you will not be able to avoid procrastinating could become a promise that fulfils itself, and causes you to procrastinate in circumstances that you might otherwise have been willing to get your work done on time.

14. A Perceived Lack Of Control

Often people procrastinate as they are powerless to monitor the consequences of events in their lives.

For example, if they feel their boss will criticize it regardless of how much effort they put into it, a person may delay getting started on an assignment at work.

While this perceived lack of control can play a role in specific, isolated cases, some people are more predisposed than others to feel a general lack of control. This issue is operationalized through the locus of control concept, which is the degree to which people believe they are in control of events in their lives. The control locus is described in an internal and external spectrum:

- Internally oriented individuals think that they have a high degree of control over their lives.

- Outside-oriented individuals believe they have a low degree of control over their lives. That external factors, such as other people or their climate, have a stronger influence over them.

- Internally oriented individuals tend to get going and finish tasks on time, while externally oriented individuals tend to procrastinate more, do poorer assignments, and feel more distressed.

15. Lack Of Motivation

People sometimes procrastinate when they don't have the time to focus on a specific mission. For example, when it comes to preparing for a test on a topic that is not important to their class, students may procrastinate, since they don't want to get a good grade.

This is often a problem when the main motivation for carrying out a task is extrinsic, as in the case of someone who is pressured by their parents to do well in school, rather than intrinsic, as in the case of someone who simply wants to feel they have learned the material successfully. Accordingly, when individuals are driven by an external source of motivation to complete a certain task, they generally show higher procrastination levels than when driven by an internal and autonomous source of motivation.

Additionally, there are many other explanations for why people may be unmotivated to function on a mission. For instance, people are unmotivated in some cases because they do not value the reward for performing the task, or because they experience a disconnection between the task they need to perform and the reward associated with it.

Finally, remember that all individuals have varying rates of overall desire for success, which implies that certain people feel more driven and inspired to accomplish their objectives in life than others are.

Many that have lower rates of incentive for success are also more prone to procrastinate on specific activities.

16. Lack of Energy

Individuals are usually more inclined to procrastinate because they suffer from poor energy levels. For example, after working hard, someone who is tiredmay find it more difficult to exercise self-control when they get home late at night, which could cause them to procrastinate on things they need to take care of like washing the dishes. In this case also, letting go Is not an option. Do whatever is in your capacity to find out what I the root-cause of your low energy level and deal with this- NOW.

17. Laziness (most common)

Laziness represents the inherent inability of an individual to render the effort required to attain their objectives, even though they may do so. In certain instances, an individual's laziness may be one of the guiding factors behind the procrastination. For example, when it comes to making the dishes, somebody might procrastinate, because they simply don't feel like getting up and doing it.

However, note that people may assume in many situations that their procrastination is driven by laziness, when it occurs due to some other underlying reason, such as anxiety or fear of failure.

Further, remember that while laziness and lack of motivation sound identical, but they are two different things. For example, it is possible for people to be strongly driven to achieve a particular objective, but at the same time not to make many strides towards this if they are unable to put in the requisite effort.

18. Prioritization of Short-Term Mood

People often procrastinate because they prioritize their feelings in the present, and do things that will help them feel better right now, even though this comes at the expense of taking action that aligns with their long-term goals, a phenomenon known as "short-term-mood-repair".

For example, a student may avoid getting started on an assignment by spending hours on tasks such as searching social media, playing video games and watching TV, since doing so in the short term is more fun than concentrating on the task.

Essentially, this type of procrastination, often referred to as hedonistic pause, happens when individuals give in to a need for quick gratification and indulge in short-term rewarding activities, rather than focusing on projects that would help them most throughout the long run.

This form of action refers to the idea of the "theory of enjoyment", which is the urge to search for pleasurable experiences and resist uncomfortable ones. While this tendency is natural and intuitive, it becomes a serious issue when a person can not control it because it causes them to pursue short-term satisfaction on an ongoing basis, at the expense of long-term achievement and development.

19. Lack Of Perseverance

Perseverance is the ability to maintain objective-driven behavior when faced with obstacles. A lack of perseverance makes people more likely to postpone, particularly when it comes to completing tasks they have already started to work on.

A lack of perseverance, for example, could cause anyone to stop working on their favorite side project because they feel they have reached a difficult and challenging development stage. Starting is good, but the ending is better.

20. Distractibility

Distractibility is the inability to concentrate your attention on one thing at a time or to stay focused overall for long. High levels or amounts of distractions can make a person more likely to procrastinate, such as when they lead people to switch constantly from one focus point to another.

For example, a person studying for a test might procrastinate because the notifications on their phone constantly distract him. Similarly, somebody might delay finishing various projects they started working on because they continue to be distracted by exciting new project ideas.

21. Sensation Seeking

Individuals often procrastinate, and they want to try and start working on assignments just before the deadline to bring motivation, difficulty, and anticipation of certain activities.

For example, a student may wait until the night before a class presentation is expected to begin working on it. They believe that doing so would make the usual dull process of planning the presentation more exciting.

This form of pause will, in certain situations, contribute to beneficial effects, such as where it motivates an individual to focus intensely on a job they might otherwise consider boring. In certain instances, though, this sort of pause contributes to adverse output consequences. However, postponing activities for this purpose may also raise the number of tension people feel, which may often hamper their output in circumstances when the interruption implies they don't have enough time to cope with any unexpected difficulties they face in their jobs.

Remember that, contrasted with preventing procrastination, some researchers refer to procrastination that happens for this cause as arousal procrastination. Nevertheless, this definition has been questioned, so knowing that from a realistic viewpoint is not important, as long as you recognize that there is a certain purpose people procrastinate.

22. High Ego And Self-esteem

Instead of being our catalysator, our, self-esteem, when too high can be a door open to postponing what we can do now, and what we actually want/need to do now because it's fully part of our talents, because we were meant to do that.

Yes, we are all gifted by God with various talents and sharing those talents- as little as they are- to bless and help others is the best way to thank Him for those gifts. Else we might end up looking down on them, murmuring because we might think the 'gift' we received is not worth 'us', that we deserve more, that we are meant for more etc. Behaving like this, there I a risk that you oversee that 'little thing' you have to make to change the world of others and start working on 'big things' that you might never end or that might end up helping nobody. This reminds me of another area of my life, which I gladly share with you in the following lines.

Like most parents that want to make the best out of their Children, my father raised us in such a way that almost every of his children should be "talented"- This kind of society or educational given "talent"- what we call "intelligence".

He motivated his children all-through and made this with great success, since each of his children was successful at school. Still, the most (and for me the only) valuable fact or result that i could personally recognize from the school educational system is the ability to make someone do the things you have to do (mostly homework, learning every kind of subjects- French, history, philosophy etc. whether you like it or not) when it has to be done, regardless if you want it or not.

For example: if the mathematic work has to be submitted on Monday, you better manage to submit it on time.

For my personal case my Father had what I call "extra big dreams", and among others He would have loved to see me working in the space at the NASA. That was his dream for me; a dream which I must admit, was fascinating to me and I embraced it also as my dream; over the years, i nourished all those big dreams , which nourished my self-esteem and overdimensioned it. And when i was thinking about my natural gifts, things that I do effortless - **cooking and writing recipes, making smoothing, doing hair braids, sewing** - i was like: "no, this kind of 'job' cannot be for me. In my country we call it serie 'C' (from French words "coiffure, couture, chomage";

To be brief, Serie C is categorized to be for uneducated people who does not know what to do in their lives. As you can imagine, this big ego and self-esteem of myself almost extinguished and killed my real passions, my natural talents. But thank God I realized it on time. I'm not trying to say one should not dream big, no. What I'm trying to say is you should manage to make your dream, your real passion, your natural talents come true, even if you are "well educated" and have the "coolest" job on the earth.

In this same context I freely start braiding the hair of my female friends when they needed it, and I was so happy to see the satisfaction and smile on their face at the end, not knowing that in this way a wide door of opportunities was opening before me as i was doing it. That is how many of those friends uncounciously advertized me, so as to bring me more clients- Even european clients- who were ready to pay for my services.

To resume this I would say all of us are talented in a unique way. We just need to recognize our capacity and fully develop our talents. When God sees you acting to deploy the gifts he has given you, He will open doors for multiplying them.

Maybe You feel like you do not know what it's your gift, your talent; Just because you does not know yet what you are talented with, doesn't mean you haven't any. The worse thing to do in this case would be to just sit down and wait; start doing something; while doing you might find it out or people may notice what you are really good in- that might be it! Try, do , exercise anything. Inspiration also does exist and will only find you while you are working, not while you are sitting.

You can start by waving to your creator and ask God where is your package (what is your talent) and "open" it (share it around you). Accept and welcome your gifts, whatever they might be. Even if it's to clean the roads or toilets, bring your ego down and just do it - true happiness definitely comes in using your natural talents to their fullest potential.

NEGATIVE EFFECTS OF PROCRASTINATION: AS A TIME, DESTINY, DREAM KILLER IF NOT CRUSHED

At any stage or another, we could feel guilty of procrastinating; nobody is a stranger to it, right? Some of us may be lucky enough to pinpoint it in time and do something about it.

The explanation of why and how we procrastinate differs from individual to individual and is not always apparent. It's also latent insecurity we don't want to accept, or it may just be as plain as not wanting to pursue it as it simply doesn't inspire us. Whatever the cause might be, be vigilant if you think you 're a procrastinator: it has much more negative consequences than you may see or understand.

Here are the seven most common effects of procrastination that not only can destroy your productivity, but also your dreams:

1. You Will Lose Precious Time

How long have you been wasting time procrastinating? Saying it is not easy, but I'm sure you can imagine. The hardest thing about procrastinating is when you remember you 're two, five, or ten years older, and nothing has improved either way. How has the entire period gone?

This is a bad feeling because the hands of time can not be turned back. You may take your time and delay, but your watch will not. There's nothing worse than feeling mad about things you should have done weeks, months, years ago, knowing that the situation might have been so different .

If you only took that first step! ...But nothing is lost: Stop saying "one day" and start making this present day the "day one", then after this "day two", etc till you reach that day called "**day end**"...upss - "**the end**".

2. You Will Blow Opportunities

How many opportunities did you waste, because when they occurred, you didn't take advantage of them? This is when you want to kick yourself truly. What you don't know is that life may have improved the chance. However, you skipped it.

Some opportunities pop about just once; a second one is not always expected. So whenever they show up, do a favor to yourself and quickly grab them with both hands!

3. You Won't Be Able To Meet Goals

When we entertain the thought of goals of wanting to achieve or change something, procrastination seems to come on with full force. You may want to change strongly, but you just don't seem to be able to take the first step forward.

That's usually really confusing and perplexing; you might think, "Why is it so hard to go for something I want so badly? "You can only answer that; you 're going to have to explore the resistance a bit deeper.

We set goals because, in some way, we have a deep desire to improve our work and actions. If you're not doing this out of procrastination, you 're sacrificing the chance to make your life easier. If it prevents you from achieving your goals, uncover the root cause behind your procrastination. Otherwise, you'll never achieve them.

4. You Could Ruin Your Career

The way you work affects your results directly, how much you accomplish, and how well you perform. Maybe procrastination will prevent you from meeting deadlines or reaching your monthly targets. What implications will this eventually have for your career?

You may lose raises or worse; you might also risk losing your work. You may continue to conceal things for a while, but don't deny that your career would almost definitely be destroyed by long-term procrastination. Don't unnecessarily discredit your results.

5. You Will Tend To Make Poor Decisions

From this standpoint, when you procrastinate and make decisions, they will almost always be poor decisions because of the place you come from (if you are not up-to-date on a topic, you won't be able to argue or even to consistently decide on anything regarding this).

If you procrastinate, you may make hative choices and decisions, as the desire to make a mature choice is not more possible as time is running out eventually.

Bad decision-taking has tremendous adverse impacts on our work quality, our productivity, our performances.

6. You Could Lower Your Reputation

If you keep saying that you are going to do something, and you are not, your reputation will inevitably get tarnished. Noone likes false claims. You harm your own credibility, as well as your esteem.

People could stop depending on you and restrain themselves from offering you opportunities because they might be worried you will just procrastinate, and they will be left to clean up the mess. A poor name has many adverse consequences that underlie it. A good reputation is preferable to money.

7. You Could Be Neglecting Your Health

Imagine if you felt your body was just not working properly, and planned to go to your doctor. Your appointment arrives, and you put it off because you felt like you worked hard all week, and you deserved a bit of rest.

You shift its thinking for yourself: "I'm not procrastinating, I am just trying to save and gain more energy by resting". Then before you realize it one day turns into a week, a week into a month, and in the end, you just forget to go.

After going out at work, you'll find you have a condition that could have been prevented if you'd just done what you needed to do.

I know someone close to me who acted on several occasions exactly as to neglect their health; That person had pain on one of her teeth and she could obtain an appointment with a dentist on a Tuesday, at

07:00 am in the morning. The day before was full of many private works and appointments, and I reached home very late that Monday and went to bed very late and tired.

On Tuesday I woke up around 5 o'clock, still feeling tired and sleepy. I deliberately decided no to go to the dentist because I wanted to sleep a bit more that morning…just for 1 or 2 more hours of sleep, I willingly and intentionally skipped my appointment, knowing very well how difficult it was to make an appointment with a dentist without a long waiting time.

One week later I started to feel the pain becoming more severe. I tried to make an appointment with several dentists- which means internet searching, calling- re-calling, etc; and the most closest one that I could obtain was in three weeks. Meanwhile it became so painful that it hindered me from going to work for three days. During those days I went to my personal doctor to have some pain-astonishing drugs. At the end, because of 1-2 hours of sleep, I ended up losing more time searching for a new appointment, which was not beneficial to my health either (if I had gone to the dentist on time, I surely would have to go through all the pains that came afterwards).

HOW TO STOP POSTPONING AND GET THINGS DONE: A SUMMARY

The sections above already mentioned some ways out of procrastination depending on the type of procrastination. This chapter will just be a summary of all of them and provide some more general solutions, with practical examples. Please note that these solutions do not have the pretension to be an exhaustive list.

How to Stop Procrastinating

Regardless of the type of procrastinator you might be, those are things you should do to come over it.

You first need to define your priorities to avoid procrastinating and then describe how pushing off can discourage you from reaching them. Next, you have to build an action plan focused on this knowledge and then execute this strategy, thereby making sure you improve it while you move along.

You'll read more about each of these measures in the following lines to use this technique as easily as possible. I will never emphasize enough on one point: Knowing the right things to do to crush procrastination won't give you victory upon it. You can know them all and still postpone the actions. Doing those things indeed and in due time is what will make you overcome.

Identify the Problem

If you wish to solve your procrastination problem successfully, it is important to understand first the exact nature of the problem you are dealing with. There are precisely three key considerations to recognize when determining the extent of the procrastination:

- **When you procrastinate:** That involves asking yourself what situations you are procrastinating in. Do you tend to procrastinate more, for example, when you work from home compared to when you're working in the library? Do you struggle to complete the tasks after starting them, or are you struggling to start in the first place?

- **How you procrastinate:** That includes telling yourself what you are doing while you procrastinate. E.g., are you searching social media, playing video games, watching TV shows, heading out with friends, or seeking to complete small and unimportant tasks?

- **Why you procrastinate:** That involves questioning yourself what causes you to procrastinate. Do you consider yourself easily disturbed, for starters, or do you feel so exhausted you don't know how to get started?

For an idea of how to take such considerations into account, envision a situation where you are taking a class where you need to turn in a set of assignments during the semester.

Each time you get a new assignment you are sitting in front of the computer in your room (the 'when'), but instead of working on the assignment you find yourself wasting time on the internet (the 'how'), because the assignment is so boring that you can't find the motivation to get started until soon before it's due (the 'why').

It's important to note that you may often end up promising yourself that you're going to get started soon, or that next time you 're going to be different in this situation. However, the same thing happened in the past, and you've never really done anything important to **change your behavior**.

The biggest explanation that occurs is that people mistakenly believe that procrastination is all about determination, while still falsely assuming that, given the facts to the contrary, they should be able to exercise more effort to alter their behavior each time.

Nevertheless, you will instead work out a rational approach to cope with it by defining the essence of your procrastination issue, rather than only believing that things will be better in the future!

Notice that the guide to procrastination psychology, which includes a detailed list of the explanations why people procrastinate, is a resource that might help you find out why you procrastinate, with the most important of these being:

- Rewards that are far in the future.

- A disconnect from your future.

- A focus on future possibilities, together with an unjustified optimism about the ability to achieve them.

- Feelings of overwhelming.

- Anxiety.

- Perfectionism.

- Fear of evaluation or negative feedback.

- Fear of failure.

- Self-handicapping.

- A perceived lack of control.

- Lack of motivation.

- Lack of energy.

- Task aversion.

- Prioritization of short-term mood.

- Distractibility.

If you're not sure why you're procrastinating, then you should read the subject guide and define the reasons for procrastination that best represent you, then come back here and figure out how to create an action plan that takes those reasons into account.

Set Your Goals

The first step toward overcoming your procrastination is setting your targets. When doing this, it's crucial to make sure your goals are as clear as possible, as you're more likely to procrastinate when it comes to vague goals than to clearly defined goals.

For starters, "getting healthy" is a fairly abstract target. You are more apt to procrastinate when it comes to achieving it than you are when it comes to following a more straightforward aim such as "drinking water and eating only unhealthy food for the next month."

Similarly, a goal such as "starting exercise" is relatively vague, and is, more likely to result in procrastination than a more concrete goal such as "going to gym three times a week and working out at least 30 minutes at a time."

You also want to make sure, when setting your goals, that those goals are achievable and meaningful:

- **'Achievable'** Signifies that the expectations will be practical enough to reach them potentially.

- **'Meaningful'** Signifies that the targets will be sufficiently significant to contribute to noticeable advancement.

For instance, writing 5,000 words each day for your thesis is meaningful, but is generally not achievable, as most people can not write at that rate, which is why such a goal should be prevented. In comparison, the goal of writing five words per day is possible, but it is not realistic, because it would take you very long to finish your research at that point, which is why that kind of target can also be prevented.

Writing 500 words per day is both achievable and meaningful in comparison, which is why it represents a good goal to set for yourself. For example, various individuals can prefer different progress levels, so there is not a single progress rate that works for everybody. As such, in your specific case, the most crucial aspect is determining the pace of change that works for you.

Overall, the first step toward overcoming your procrastination is setting your targets. These objectives should be simple, realistic, and important, implying they should be well-defined, realistic, and sufficiently relevant to help you make noticeable progress.

You will continue on to the next phase in this cycle after you set your targets, which is to define the exact essence of your procrastination issue.

Create A Plan Of Action

If you have established your objectives and defined the essence of your struggle with procrastination, you will develop an action plan that will encourage you to avoid procrastinating and start doing stuff.

You need to figure out which anti-procrastination techniques to use and how to use them to create an action plan. These techniques, listed in the next section, fall into two principal categories:

- **Behavioral Techniques:** Such strategies include manipulation of your acts explicitly, allowing you to instill healthy attitudes and prevent harmful ones. Examples of anti-procrastination coping strategies include splitting major projects into smaller ones and eliminating obstacles from work settings.

- **Cognitive Techniques:** These techniques involve a direct modification of your thoughts, helping to avoid thinking of excuses you will give if you don't act and focusing on the satisfaction of things accomplished.

Generally speaking, every technique should likely help you achieve at least one of the following things:

- **Make it easier for you to get started:** For instance, leaving the document you need to work on open on your computer before you go to sleep will make it easier for you to start working on it once you sit down at the computer the following day.

- **Make it easier for you to keep going once you've started:** For starters, having your phone in quiet mode and out of reach decreases the risk that alerts can interrupt you when you're working, making it simpler to focus on your job.

- **Make it harder for you to avoid working:** Turning off the WiFi on your device and phone, for example, would eliminate the urge to procrastinate on social media instead of writing your article.

Whatever variety of techniques you choose, use the ones that match you better in the specific circumstance, because various strategies can function differently on different individuals, and function differently in different circumstances with the same person.

As such, be sure to identify the nature of your procrastination problem before deciding which techniques to use to solve it.

Later, once you feel more comfortable with the situation, you can choose to implement additional techniques or to skip some of them if you wish.

MOST GENERAL AND COMMON ANTI-PROCRASTINATION TECHNIQUES

Please note that this list has no pretention to be exhaustive.

1. Break Large Tasks Into Smaller Ones

Breaking big tasks into smaller sub-tasks will motivate you to take action, making big tasks seem less daunting, and encouraging you to enjoy a constant stream of satisfying progress. Also, doing so benefits you from an organizational perspective. It helps you identify what you need to do to achieve your goals, and make plans that include a high level of detail.

2. Prioritize Tasks

Prioritizing your tasks can help you figure out which tasks to perform and when to perform. This will ensure that you do not end up procrastinating by wasting time on trivial tasks while neglecting important ones. It will also help you avoid situations where you feel overwhelmed because you are not sure where to start, or which tasks you should be working on.

Two common ways of prioritizing your tasks are as follows:

- The Ivy Lee method. This method involves preparing a to-do list at the end of each day and writing down a list of six tasks, ranked in order of importance, that you will want to complete tomorrow.

- The Eisenhower Matrix. This method involves categorizing each task you have based on whether it is important or not, whether it is urgent or not, and then prioritizing your tasks based on those criteria.

Overall, there are many methods that you can use to make your tasks a priority. Do not spend time over-optimizing the system of prioritization or lost finding out which one to use; just pick one to start with and then test other approaches before you figure out which one fits well.

3. Identify Your Productivity Cycles

Various persons have specific activity patterns that ensure various people are successful at different periods of the day. Some people might work better in the morning, for example, while others might be more productive in the evenings. Similarly, certain individuals can be the most efficient after eating, and others might be more successful while starving.

A smart way to that the propensity to procrastinate is to recognize the busiest hours, which are the hours of the day that you 're most successful, and then to arrange the day such that much of the work is planned for certain days.

Ultimately, when planning for the work periods, bear in mind that you can be able to do various activities easier at certain hours of the day. For instance, because it is still early in the day, you may be able to do creative tasks easier, and menial tasks easier when it is fairly late.

4. Establish A Routine

It may be good to create a regular daily/weekly / monthly schedule to enable you to stop procrastinating.

For example, you can set up a creative work routine early in the morning before checking out emails or social media, which is a good way to make sure you start your day productive, and by completing your most important tasks while you're still in a clear mind.

5. Set Deadlines For Yourself

Setting deadlines on your own will reduce the probability of procrastinating because deadlines act as a communication tool that lets you prepare ahead and encourage yourself.

There are some items you can bear in mind when setting time limits for yourself:

- Deadlines should be concrete: As we have shown before, you are more inclined to follow through with concretely established commitments than follow through with abstract commitments. E.g., this implies that "Thursday at 4 pm" is a stronger deadline than "Tomorrow at some point."

- Deadlines should be realistic: You will pick deadlines that will allow you as much time as you need to complete a mission, but no more.

- Deadlines should be meaningful: Deadlines are only beneficial if you actually adhere to them, so your deadline should be set in such a way as to encourage you to follow them through.

It's also important to remember that deadlines should prompt you to start early work. Therefore you should avoid using deadlines, which encourage you to wait until the last possible minute to get your work started.

7. Use Time-Management Techniques

You can use various time-management methods to make it easy for you to get going with your job and remain centered once you have begun.

You may do the Pomodoro Method, for example, a time-management strategy where you use a timer to coordinate the workflow. Pomodoro Method includes operating for a fixed time (e.g., 25 minutes) on the assignments and then having a brief rest (e.g., 5 minutes) before beginning to work again. Additionally, after you reach a certain amount of work periods (e.g., 4 hours) as part of the Pomodoro, you will take a longer break (e.g., 30 minutes) before you return to work.

This technique and similar ones can be modified to suit your personal preferences. For example, you might opt to use a particular metric instead of a certain time to restrict the increasing work process by utilizing the Pomodoro method, such as the number of words you have written or the number of pages you have read.

With anyone, not one approach fits exactly; you can pursue various methods before you find the one that works with you. If you're unsure which one to begin with, just go for the Pomodoro Technique and change it as you move along.

8. Use A To-Do List

Using a to-do list is extremely useful in helping you avoid procrastinating, for several reasons:

- It helps you break down your goals into actionable tasks.

- It helps you organize your tasks, prioritize them, and optimally schedule them.

- It helps you focus only on specific tasks that you need to be thinking of at the moment.

- It helps you write down deadlines and stick with them.

- It helps you track your progress and figure out what works for you and what doesn't.

Test multiple strategies before you find the one that fits well for you, but as always, make sure you don't get caught over-optimizing stuff, and just pick one choice to continue with at first. You can always reassess the situation if necessary, and modify your solution as you go along.

9. Gamify Your Behavior

Gamification requires the integration of features from sports, such as rivalry with others and collection of points, into certain forms of tasks to improve the desire to function for the goals. Gamification may be an effective method when properly applied when it comes to helping yourself to avoid procrastinating.

10. Reward Yourself For Your Accomplishments

Every single step counts. Remember those days where you were still procrastinating and reward yourself after each measurable achievement/improvement. Rewards should be given for meaningful behaviors to allow you to make progress, but that is also sufficiently accessible to motivate you in the short run.

For example, you may opt to take a brief break and watch some Television for any chapter you read in preparation for a report, or you can enjoy a little slice of candy as a treat for any job you perform when working on a project.

12. Commit To Having No Zero Days

As I say in a previous chapter, stop counting days and making each day count.

A zero-day is a day where you are making almost little strides in all of your goals. You can commit to no longer having zero-days, by choosing not to end your day until you manage to take at least one step towards reaching one of your goals, even if it's just a minor one, like writing a single paragraph or going out for a five-minute walk.

This strategy will give you a good motivating boost and inspire you to follow your goals continuously.

14. Increase your energy level

Increasing your energy levels is one of the best ways to get out of the slumps and get you to stop procrastinating, as being tired can increase your chances of procrastinating.

Specifically, some of the key things you can do to increase your energy levels are as follows:

- **Get enough sleep:** If you don't get enough sleep, you 're more apt to procrastinate. So, only making sure you sleep adequately would enable you to be more successful and improve your overall well-being.

- **Drink some water.** When it comes to your capacity to focus on your job, fatigue is a major concern, and you can quickly fix it by only consuming a glass of water from time to time. Certain beverages are somewhat appropriate, but try not to eat too much caffeine or sugar, which may cause the energy rates to drop for a bit.

- **Eat (moderately) healthy.** When you are hungry, consume something that will give you the strength you need. Stop fast foods or treats that can boost your appetite for a limited period and leave you to feel sluggish afterward.

- **Take a break and go outside.** When you're trapped all day indoors and sense the walls close around you, take a quick break to go outside and enjoy some new air and clear your mind.

- **Get some exercise.** Not need to repeat how benefical exercising can operate on our body and physical well-beeing.

15. Improve Your Work Environment

A bad working environment can cause you to delay more, while a good working environment can help you to be more productive. You will also seek to change the work experience as much as possible by having it a position where you can comfortably concentrate on the job. For e.g., if your desk becomes so cluttered that it becomes impossible for you to focus on reading your homework, that might render you more vulnerable to disturbances and thus to procrastinate too.

16. Change Your Work Location

If you find that when you try to get it done at a certain location, you are more likely to procrastinate on your work, go elsewhere when you want to work.

For starters, when you're attempting to work on the computer in your home, if you can't get yourself to quit procrastinating, then go to the library or coffee shop and work there instead.

17. Eliminate (unnecessary) Distractions

Removing (unnecessary) disruptions from life ensures that you would be more able to concentrate on the job and prevent procrastination.

Example, if your phone emits a noisy sound any time you get a message, you will be continuously annoyed when you're working, which would make it harder for you to concentrate. In these cases, you'll want to place your phone in quiet mode when you're operating or using special software to hide alerts to help you focus on your job.

You should bear in mind, when doing this, the harmful influence that even apparently minor distractions can have on you.

18. Make It Harder For Yourself To Procrastinate

The harder you make it for yourself to engage in procrastinatory behaviors, the better you can avoid procrastinating.

For starters, if you intend to compose a paper on your desktop and you want to procrastinate by searching social media, disabling the places you normally look at when procrastinating would make it easier for you to procrastinate. It would improve the chances of you going to work substantially, purely because there's little more for you to do.

19. Make It Easier To Get Started On Tasks

The quicker you find to get going on the projects you need to do, the more likely you will have them done promptly.

For example, if you decide to focus on a particular paper, then you should keep it open on your computer when you go to sleep so that it's the first thing you'll see when you turn on your machine in the morning, which improves the probability that you'll be focused on it.

20. Make Unpleasant Tasks More Enjoyable

Typically speaking, the more stressful a certain job becomes, the more often you can procrastinate. As such, by finding stressful jobs more appealing, you are reducing the possibility of procrastinating.

There are many ways that you can make the tasks more attractive. For example, if you need to clean the house, you can put on the music you like and try to find out how much you can do in a 10-minute sprint of work to make this otherwise boring task more enjoyable.

21. Minimize The Number Of Decisions You Have To Make

For example, if you need to write a paper, you can create a timeline of which portions of the paper you need to work on in advance, so you don't have to decide what to do each day. Likewise, just before you go to sleep, you should choose the clothes you'll wear the next day, which would stop you from making a choice just before you continue the day.

Therefore, remember that the more choices you have to select before choosing what to do, the easier it would be for you to make a choice and the more likely you are to procrastinate. As such, you can reduce the likelihood that you'll procrastinate by minimizing the number of options you can choose from.

22. Set Time Constraints For Decision-Making

When you want to procrastinate, and you are unable to make choices in a timely fashion, you will restrict the time available to you to make decisions by giving yourself arbitrary time limits.

23. Start With Your Best Or Worst Tasks

Many people consider it helpful to continue their day by tackling the thing they 're most fearful of because they can get it out of the way quickly, and move through the remainder of the day, thinking they've already taken care of it.

24. Start With A Tiny Step

Deciding to commit to just a tiny step can sometimes help you get started on tasks you 're procrastinating on, particularly when you're procrastinating because the task somehow feels overwhelming or scary.

25. Immediately Complete Small Tasks

One strategy to stop waiting for tiny projects is only to have them finished as soon as you figure out you need to do them whenever you do. It has the additional benefit of keeping such minor activities from adding up before they are daunting, which is also much more effective than spending time later arranging certain activities.

26. Switch Between Tasks

When you're focused on something, or sound lost, try jumping into a new job for a bit before moving to the initial activities you've been procrastinating.

Doing so is advantageous even though it will preferably be easier for you to focus on the original mission, because it is safer to do anything less significant than doing none at all, and because moving between tasks at your discretion will allow you "unstuck" when it is time to return to the original task.

27. Figure Out What You're Afraid Of

People often procrastinate because they fear something, whether it is doing badly on a task or obtaining negative feedback from other people. Identifying the reason you 're worried about a task can help you cope with your fear, which can help you get your work started.

For example, if you realize that you're predisposed to starting a new hobby because you're worried you're going to embarrass yourself, you can talk to people in the community to address this fear, which will help you get started.

28. Avoid A Perfectionist Mindset

Perfectionism, which is the inclination in one's job to aim for the flawlessness, may lead people to procrastinate in many ways:

- Perfectionism will lead you to postpone getting going since you are afraid you may not be able to do perfect results.

- Perfectionism can cause you to continue endlessly revising your work because you are still finding minor flaws in your work.

- Perfectionism may lead you to stop revealing your work or making it public because you are worried it isn't perfect at all.

The first move in coping with this problem is to recognize that you are procrastinating because of your perfectionism. When you are conscious that this is a challenge, you have to internalize the idea that your job is okay not to be completely perfect, and that you cannot let your fear of having an error trigger you to procrastinate.

For example, if the issue is that you can't really get going, then you have to embrace the reality that at first, the job would still have some flaws. Try to get something done even if, during this initial stage, it is of low quality and remember that you can always improve it later.

Similarly, if your concern is that you keep revising your work constantly or delay publishing your work, you can ask for input from the experienced people you trust, who can give you an objective appraisal of the content of your work, and inform you if it is ready to be released, and if not, what changes you need to make.

In fact, you should always ask yourself what the repercussions of publishing work that is not completely flawless are, and then follow that up by telling yourself how severe such effects are, and whether they compare against the possible advantages of actually putting the work out there.

29. Forgive Yourself For Past Procrastination

Forgiving yourself for previous cases of procrastination in the future will motivate you to procrastinate less. For example, research reveals that when it came time to prepare for later tests, students who forgave themselves for procrastinating on previous exams procrastinated less.

Remember, though, not forgiving yourself could lead you to lack the motivation you need to improve.

30. Develop Self-Efficacy And A Positive Outlook

Self-efficacy is the belief in your capacity to carry out the necessary actions to achieve your goals. This confidence is essential to your willingness to self-regulate your behavior, which helps you stop procrastinating effectively.

Self-efficacy is strongly linked to being hopeful and having a positive outlook on your situation, which in some cases can also help to reduce your tendency to procrastinate by doing things like increasing your motivation to work and reducing your fear of failure.

Two key forms of thought include remaining hopeful:

- Pathway thinking. It reflects the belief that you will use methods to address your problems.

- Agency thinking. This represents the belief that the strategies that can be used to solve your problems can be successfully pursued.

You can do this by doing things like going over your past successes in your mind and remembering that even if you have made mistakes in the past, you have learned from them and are now better equipped to deal with obstacles you might encounter.

It is also important, however, to remain realistic when it comes to your self-efficacy and optimism, and to avoid allowing them to cause you to shy away.

31. Focus On The Goal Instead Of On The Task

For starters, if you're procrastinating on an assignment because it's tedious, try not to worry about the job itself while you're struggling to motivate yourself to do the work, but instead talk about the fundamental purpose for wanting to do it, if it's about having a good score, receiving a raise, or simply being able to relax without feeling guilty.

32. Find Someone Who Can Hold You Accountable

Finding a friend or a parent who can keep you responsible for your acts in certain circumstances will help you avoid procrastinating.

Whether it's a teacher, a colleague, a parent, or a friend, the person who holds you accountable can be anyone you trust. The better they can hold you accountable, the more their help motivates you to do your work in a timely fashion.

Note that there need not necessarily be any tangible reward or penalty involved in the way the other person holds you accountable; if you care enough about their opinion about you, sometimes even wanting them to be proud of your actions or wanting to avoid deceiving them can be all the motivation you need.

33. Seek Favorable Peer Influence

The people you spend time with can greatly impact your ability to avoid procrastinating. There are two main things you should do, to account for this:

Seek positive peer influence. That means you should try to spend time with people who influence you well. For example, this includes people who work hard, pursue their goals, hold themselves accountable for their actions, and encourage you to do the same.

Avoid negative peer influence. That means you can want to reduce the amount of time you 're spending with others who have a negative effect on you. For example, this includes people who waste their time, neglect their goals, and never take responsibility for their actions and encourage you to do the same.

34. Build A Social Support Network

A social support network is a group of people you can count on to provide you with emotional, informational, and practical assistance. A close friend or a study partner, for example, are two types of people you could include in your social support network.

In certain instances, social encouragement may help to minimize procrastination. For example, if you're procrastinating because you're afraid of failing at anything, talking to someone on your social support network could help you conquer your fear.

Note that the support network's existence or scale might not be important, as long as you have the resources you need.

In addition, note that in some cases, you can also benefit from having a significant personal network that includes people who share your situation in some way but don't necessarily expect you to support them. For E.g., your peers in the classroom or at work could also be considered part of your network.

35: Do It Today- Or Someone Else will

I cannot express this better if it is not with these following, personal experiences:

- In 2014, as I was still a student, I wanted to create a snackery in my country. I had a pretty clear idea of how I wanted it to be and which products I wanted to propose to my clients, but I did nothing more than drafting those ideas on a mindmap. My first reason (or first excuse) was to finish at university first, and the second "reason" was that I did not have money for that anyway. One year later, in 2015 I was finally graduated but still- I did nothing about my project. In January 2018, more than three years later, I was upset to meet during a festival in my town a second semester student launching his company with exactly the idea of snackery that I had in mind four years ago. As I was talking with him, I could notice he had less ressources than me 3 years ago to launch his business. I'll better skip how I felt - but of course I was happy for him and was also challenged to see people who truly dare.

- The second short story: I noticed that in my country, many use imported (mainly from Europe) liquid soaps for their household, which is very costly for most of the population. I thought about producing it in my country , mainly with ashes, which can be easily and cheaply produced or collected there. I draw a very good business model of how the ashes could be collected from my dreamed "snackery" as many snacks would have been fried using wood, which would result in ashes. But after that, due to the postponing mood I was in, I took absolutely no other action, no first step to start that although I could. A month later, I discovered in social medias a young lady who had just launched that business, and it was running very well. I have many more examples of projects that I could not (dare to) launch, which I see people around me realize.

By this time, I realized the real problem was overthinking, the fear to get out of my comfort zone, and the wish to wait for that "perfect time" to do that "perfect thing".

Definitely if you don't act, if you don't do "it", someone else will.

Make a decision today. Make a choice. it's fully your choice to start acting, to start making steps forwards. If you do not make any choice, neither to start or not to start, that itself will still be a choice – and the worse one.

One painful truth is, the average human life is relatively short; another is, you own just the present. So please- "Do it now", tomorrow might be too late!

CONCLUSION

If you're grappling with procrastination, the road you 're on doesn't have to end. You don't have to feel that way if you feel like your life is a complete train wreck because you keep procrastinating. And understanding the causes of procrastination is one of the most important things you can do to overcome those feelings. This is the number one secret that will stop procrastinating.

Because most people think laziness, stubbornness, and generally being bad are the causes of procrastination. As long as you think you're procrastinating because of who you are, because you're not that good or apt, because you want to or are lazy and worthless, you can't make any progress towards stopping procrastination. The causes of procrastination have to be understanding.

There are several reasons for shifting tasks and none of them is linked to your behavior. They have to do with what you hear, and with what you face. And this will alter you. Fear is one of the major factors in procrastination. This can be a fear of performance and success, fear of failure, or some uncertain, unreasonable distress. The fact is these fears are capable of creating procrastination and keeping you stuck.

Another of the major causes is overcome by procrastination. Having so much gone on is very easy, that we just don't know what to do next. We might know many things that could be accomplished, so we procrastinate as long as we don't have the next step in mind. Other causes of procrastination include sickness and fatigue. Yet laziness is not one of the primary causes of procrastination. You might believe you're lazy, and that's why you're procrastinating.

But the truth is because you procrastinate, you'll feel lazy. Fatigue is not the source; it is the consequence. If you understand the causes of procrastination, you will move ahead in avoiding procrastination and living your life the way you want to live. The best news is you don't have to fight off procrastination and feel like your life is a train wreck. Just knowing what's going on can get you much closer to overcoming procrastination and being more successful.

Do Not Go Yet; One Last Thing To Do

If you enjoyed this book or found it useful, I'd be very grateful if you'd post a short review on Amazon.

Publishing this book is also something that I pushed off several times- waiting for the perfect time, the perfect words, the perfect season to post it out. But finally it's out- Yeahh!

Your comments and even critics will surely make a difference.

I will read all the reviews personally so I can get your feedback and make this book even better.

Thanks for your help and support!

Made in the USA
Middletown, DE
01 May 2022

65054442R00066